MW01490714

Be Unf**kwithable:

A Practical Guide on How to Own Life

MXXV

Introduction:

- **Unfuckwithable: An individual who cannot and will not be fucked with. This individual is usually unstoppable and is never threatened by anyone. It's also a state of mind; in your mind you need to be number 1, you need to never allow someone else to shake your own confidence.**

I want to preface this book with this description: this is not a motivational or a self-help nor even an uplifting book, look at more as a guide, how to live or even if you choose, how not to live. And truth be told, it is not a great book, I am honest, it is my first attempt, but I will say that hopefully it is a thoughtful read. I may get off topic or stray from the point of each chapter, and I will repeat myself, sorry if that gets annoying. But I will try to incorporate, anytime I can, a story about my own meandering experience, as a friend, a man, a dad, a son, or as a teacher.

Now I'm no public speaker, and this is my first attempt at writing a book (it's not my first idea, but my first time I actually sat down and said "where do I start"), I'm honestly nothing more than a guy who has done a fair share of reading, and I like to think of myself as a pretty well-rounded human. I'm also a nice guy, although you shouldn't have to announce to the world, you're nice, the world should see that, but one thing I've learned through my own trials and tests in life is to never let your niceness be a weakness. You can still be a nice a person, and demand to be treated accordingly. I like to think of myself as someone who will give you the shirt of my back but also be able to tell someone to go to hell in the same time frame. Basically, how to be unfuckwithable, is for when a person is unwilling to tolerate others screwing up their homeostasis (that's a science term for maintaining your balance) - these are the most dangerous type of people in the world.

You're not being mean, rude, or wrong if you demand to be treated well. You should learn to command respect from others rather than demanding it. You do not necessarily have to be the boss to be able to take charge, sometimes it the most unsuspecting person who is the real leader. And what really is a leader, it's a person who refuses to accept anything less than the best from themselves, and who refuses to accept nothing but the best from those around them and who wants nothing but the best for those that are around as well. In my younger years I was once placed in a managerial position at a local municipal pool. I had lifeguards and pool attendants who worked under me. I lived by two rules as their boss:

1) Never ask an employee to do something you yourself haven't already done, or you aren't willing to do yourself

2) If your employees are working harder than you, there's a problem

As a true leader, a truly unfuckwithable person, if you treat employees (and in all reality all people) well, they will do anything for you, without hesitation. I've had to clean up the worst things you could imagine working at this pool, my staff saw and knew I did this work, so when I asked them to do it, they complied – but I would also reward them , maybe it was an extra break or they could leave early without a docked pay. And at the end of the day or the end of their shift, I would always thank them for a great day – I had two lifeguards who literally wouldn't leave until they heard me say that, because it made them feel accomplished and appreciated.

You will be many different people to others – no one will ever get the exact same version. Some people will look at me as the epitome of everything in this book, and others will say I'm nothing like these ideas. What really matters in long run is how you see yourself. Being unfuckwithable, isn't a physical state, it's more a mindset. These people have their own control under control, meaning they will never allow another person to shake their confidence (that means you Cecilia, I haven't forgotten what you did to Paul.) I'm no "alpha" male, I don't like sports, my knowledge of cars is very limited and I hate the term "man-cave." To some, this would lower my "man-card" status, and to them I direct them to my hand that is presenting to them my middle finger. Unfuckwithability has nothing to do with male or female, nor race or age or anything that can separate or divide people. Anyone can be unfuckwithable, the choice is up to you where you leave the control. Remember to some you might be an average person – nothing special; but to others you might just be looked at as a god – don't ever disappoint these people.

If you find motivation or you are uplifted by this book, that is great and I thoroughly encourage you to share your thoughts, and any newfound knowledge with as many people as you can. This book is nothing more than a series of pieces of advice or sayings, or god knows I hate but clichés; that I do not take full credit for writing all. Some are from my deep philosophical side, so if there is one that has no "author unknown", then that is in fact my own saying. Others are things I read on the internet, where no author is given credit. If you are the author of one of these quotes, I would like to give you my fullest respect and appreciations, but for Christ sakes get off your ass and get on the net and make sure that you find the sites using your work and get your goddam due credit. In an earlier draft of this book, I did incorporate a large number of pop culture references – from movies, tv and music, but unfortunately due to copyright laws I wasn't able to obtain permission for a large number of them, and in all honesty, by desire to not be sued slightly outweighed my desire to publish this book the way I had intended. Any quotes that do have an author, after much research, do fall under "public domain" but out of respect I tried to give full and proper r credit.

You will read things in this book that you may like, you'll probably read things you won't, but honestly, I don't care what you think, I care more about the fact that you are at least thinking. I encourage you to do more of that, *thinking*, because if you are paying, at least a little bit of attention, thinking and thinkers are becoming an "endangered species" because fewer and fewer people are doing it. True thinkers are truly unfuckwithable. People do not think any more, they like to repeat what they have heard, change a few words around, and think it is their own thought. Don't be the douche with the ponytail from the bar scene in "Good Will Hunting," for any millennial readers, "Good Will Hunting" is a spectacular movie about life and how true knowledge really comes from the experiences of life rather than texts from a book, and I highly recommend watching it, and yes I do see the irony in being told in a book, to get your head out of book or movie and live life. Also, I hope you will re-read this book. You may read it now and nothing strikes a chord with you. You will read it again later in life and then things might make sense. Again, I hope if anything, this book gets you to think, and to think beyond your comfort zone. Read things you like, but also read things you do not like or read things that you disagree with. This is the first step of being open minded. If you are enthusiastic about your beliefs, it would be foolish to think others are enthusiastic about theirs. Learn to communicate with them, have a conversation, and understand that it is acceptable to agree to disagree. Just because you disagree with someone does not mean you have to hate them.

"There are going to be people who hate you, so you better give them a hell of a good reason"

Keep thinking, before it becomes illegal, because it is already not cool, - not cool to be well informed.

It is just as sucky to be misinformed as it is to be uniformed-write that down. And, there a difference between being misinformed and being uninformed, but both are terrible mind sets but as the old adage goes, ignorance is bliss. Now you may have been offended by that statement, and if you are, good, maybe it got you thinking, maybe you can start learning to listen and comprehend an idea. People are too soft, they are offended by anyone who had a different opinion from theirs, because as we have been raised to believe, we are always right and everyone else is always wrong. These are the same people who think others are being mean or rude, just because they are not stroking their fragile ego. Now I'm not saying I'm any better than anyone else, I may be a jerk and have high self-esteem, but I'm not arrogant like that, I talk a lot of smack, but I can back it up. There's always a very fine line to dance on between arrogance and confidence, just never forget which side your dancing; if you aren't sure maybe speak with someone, a close friend is a good choice, but maybe a better one would be someone who you aren't particularly close with or fond of, they'll probably give you more of an unbiased answer.

What I am also saying is I can handle the truth and so should you. People need to respect the truth, even if they don't like it, and hell I haven't always like hearing the truth, but everyone needs to be "called out" or put "in check" every once in a while. You get complacent with life and nothing changes. Nothing changes nothing, so if you are miserable in your environment, if you do not change something, you get to continue being miserable.

"Don't advertise everything you do. People cannot destroy what they don't know"

Always have a plan, but do not live a life where all you do is live to plan. Live in this moment because this very moment is something you cannot ever get back. Time is always fleeting and the next moment is never promised to anyone. "Now" never exists, we are always in a constant state of the past or the immediate future

Read forth and take notes, develop a thought or idea of your own and share it with people, with friends, with strangers, just share it. Knowledge is power, and sharing it is the highest form of wealth, at least to me it is. One final note before you start this book, a lot of the ideas overlap from chapter to chapter, so please don't be surprised if you think you're having Deja vu, because more than likely I have repeated myself, also there will probably be plenty of contradictions throughout the chapters, but guess what that's life. Contradictions occur everywhere,: An environmentalist may preach against carbon emissions, but chances are they used a gas car or airplane to get places; a medieval knight who fought in the Crusade would preach kindness and peace but then slaughter enemies who stood in his way; A CEO will talk about improving the lives of their employees while still utilizing sweat shops in

China. The world is full of opposing thought processes, so please forgive any you read in this book.... I hope you can win at life. Enjoy!!!

Chapter 1

Only those who will risk going too far can possibly find out how far one can go - George Eliot
You can do more than you think. Push yourself.

So, you want to be unfuckwithable, you want to be winner at life. You read the intro, now let's get right to it. What really makes a person unfuckwithable? Unfuckwithable people are not always super bad ass tough guys, we aren't action movie stars and we are not infallible. We have a mindset that won't allow other to shake us, and if somehow, we get shaken, we regroup, adapt and make sure the other person gets shaken harder. We don't win every fight, physical or by word, but dammit when others see or talk to our opponent, they can see, clear as day, that the other person was in a fight. Unfuckwithability goes beyond male and female or age; you stand up for what you believe, even if that makes you unpopular, and you're unapologetic about it– but when you have wronged or hurt someone you aren't afraid to apologize and make amends. Sorry means nothing in this world, we are conditioned to immediately say sorry when we know we did something wrong. A theme you'll read several times in this book is that actions speak louder than words – you can't just say you're sorry, you have to show it and actually mean it.

They (We) make mistakes, they screw up, they can't live up to every point made in this book. When we fall, usually we are the first to laugh at ourselves (there is a big difference between being laughed with and being laughed at – the prior feels great, the latter no so much) but we are always our own worst critic. Humans have the innate ability to want to make others feel good, but have no problem putting ourselves down. Now the idea of self-deprecating humor is always fun, but one must remember is that that is fine, if it's only for entertainment and should never reflect a true sense of your own worth. If you lower your own worth, what's to say the rest of the world won't do the same?

Life is not a race, if it is then the finish line is your grave, and I for one am not in any rush to get there, I highly or hopefully doubt any one is. But for the sake of playing devil's advocate, if you must look at it like a race, then guess who your only competition is - I'll give you one hint, go look in the mirror. The only person you need to outdo is the person looking back at you in the reflection, YOU. You can always do more, have better, go farther, but you'll never see your potential or understand your capability until you let go of any preconceived notions you have about yourself and just go for it. Give it your all, even if nobody else is watching or even if nobody else even cares. Be unfuckwithable!!!!

If you are always thinking about your best, and complaining that you are the only one giving it your all, then here's a wakeup call, you aren't actually doing anything at all!!! If you have to energy to complain, then that's energy wasted on going further than you thought.

No one cares when you win, but they'll always remember when you lose, and they'll remind you all the time, just in case you forget. That goes for everything and everyone – Who won best actor/actress at the 2006 Academy Award, no cheating, I don't know and I'm sure all hell sure you don't know either? Who got the gold in Bobsledding at the Beijing Olympics – not that bobsledding is the go-to event that everyone needs to watch? Never be afraid to celebrate your own success, you have to be your biggest fan. And don't be afraid to make sure others know you are celebrating their success- since you can't be their biggest fan, definitely try to be there number 2. And on that note, keep your circle small. Those in your circle should be the ones cheering loudest for your success – they should want to see you succeed. But they should also be the ones to help hold you up during your failures. If your circle doesn't do this, the answer is simple: You need a new circle (write that down.)

When you cease to take chances then you'll cease to live. Here's a little riddle for you, "What are the two most dangerous words in the world? ". Any idea, they are "what if.... " What if I don't take that job, what if I don't ask her /him out, what if, what if, what if. In this life we always have at least three choices: give up, give or give it your all. Not everything is always work out for the best for us, that's life – you can either dwell on that and be full of "what if's" or embrace the failure, see where you need to improve and move on. Don't be afraid of failure, actually welcome it. Know that every time you fail, that means you are going to be one step closer to success. Apply this to your whole life. As a young guy I was rejected and reject by many women- it really started to wear on me, I just kept getting shot down, then finally I met a girl who actually was interested and we had a wonderful relationship. I keep this one in mind because if it hadn't been for all of the other rejections, I wouldn't have met her and she wouldn't have helped make me who I am. Each failure is chance to improve, get better, make and embrace a change, and if you do this, I promise you will get to where you want to be. And be the one who can always keep their cool. Don't let the stresses of the world bring you down. You can't control everything, so why freak out over things you cannot change.

"Well, well, well...if it isn't the consequences of my own actions. So, we meet again..." ~ Unknown

Our decisions shape who we are, for good or bad. You cannot have regrets about the things you have done, things you should've done or things you wish would have happened. You will be hurt by others when you didn't deserve to be, and you will hurt others, when they didn't deserve it. You will be loved and hated for reasons that are crystal clear and for reasons you cannot fathom. So just remember that because these instances occurred or hadn't, who you are at this very moment would not be the person you were meant to be, which in the grand scheme of it all, is ultimately the most perfect version of you. If you don't think you aren't the best version of yourself right, well you're wrong. If you weren't perfect for this very moment, nature or the universe wouldn't have made you present for it.

You can drive yourself crazy always trying to figure things out and replay scenes in your head, about what would have been different if you had taken that chance, if you had pushed yourself. You cannot change the past, I know I've thought about it, I'm not happy with all the decisions I've made, the people I've hurt, the things I've ruined, but if I hadn't made those choices, would I have had this moment right here right now - to answer that, I have to say I don't know. I don't know what would have happened if I made that left instead of that right, or if I had left the party 1 hour earlier or 1 hour later, had I picked up the phone instead of hitting decline. The fact of the matter is you won't know, there is no secretive reset button, all you can do is own your choices and accept the fact that if you don't push forward, you'll always stay in the same place. And for some, that one place will be fine, and they will be content with having what they have. But if you truly believe that you were meant for more, then damn it, go for it.

Life is just too short. If you are reading this and you are a young person, savor every moment, because in your life, you are young for a very small amount of time. You're old for a vast majority of your time on earth. Go out and get out of your comfort zone. If you don't, you will not have a great story to share when you are old. Again, as mention in the intro, the theme behind "Good Will Hunting" is to enjoy the experiences of life, first hand – don't spend all you time reading about the Grand Canyon, go see it for yourself. Don't live an Instagram life and don't envy those who do; they only show the best parts or the parts that they were able to get the perfect photo of – you don't see the 75 deleted pictures. Unfuckwithable people don't live an edited life, they enjoy the bad photos just as much as the good ones. They don't need to have 25 photos taken of themselves before they find the right one – because if you think you are fat or ugly in one picture, changing a pose or angle isn't going to change that – only your mind set will do that. Confidence is key with unfuckwithability and owning life. And when you finally own your life, you will win at life.

At the end of everything, look at who you are, and would you want to be friends with yourself, or would you want your children to be like you or be friends with someone like you. You must be the hero of your own story, because nobody else should be taking that role, if they are, then guess what it was never your story in the first place.

Chapter 2

Friends, some are meant to just be part of the supporting cast, while others have starring roles.

      The term friend has become a very meaningless word. Social media has you being friends with people you've never met, just because they liked your post. We have confused friends with followers. A true friend isn't a follower, but will follow you into hell and back. Your friends and who you surround yourself with, ultimately can make or break your level of unfuckwithability. You have to surround yourself with those who inspire you, and likewise who you must inspire. If the people you are with don't make you "up" your game, then why do you keep them around. At the same time if you realize that a friend no longer is around, maybe they finally saw that you aren't making them better. It's all about bettering yourself and those around you, if you aren't, why are you waking up in the morning.

Loyalty always defines friendships. And you need to be loyal to a fault, because the dream is that your friend (s) will return the same level. Your family isn't necessarily defined by blood, family can emerge through a shared experience, albeit a positive moment or even a negative. Sometimes our darkest times help lay the foundations of our strongest bonds.

Your friends have a power over you, let me explain. It doesn't matter how you think other people see you, they will see the company you keep. If you surround yourself with undesirable people, i.e. low life scum, guess how the world will seed you, lie life scum. Your company will directly impact the energy that you give to the world, so if you would like to be seen as a self-respected individual, then you need to surround yourself with people that also exclude that impression.

"There will come a time in your life when you will become infatuated with a single soul. For this person you would do anything and not think twice about it, but when asked why, you will have no answer. You will try your whole life to understand how a single person can affect you as much as they do, but still you will find no answer. And no matter how badly you hate it or how badly it will hurt, you'll love this person without regret for the rest of your life." – unknown

This is one of my all-time favorite quotes about love, but as I have grown over the years, I've seen how this can be applied to not only a romantic love (which I still have a place for it in regard to romance, in my heart) but to the love you have for your friends. Obviously, some of the words in the quote refer to romance, but let's change some things, maybe the words infatuated or love can be replaced with a sense of unexplainable respect or simple adoration. We all have "our people." Those that seem to have always been there and then some who come to you out of the blue. But no matter how they came to you, you both know you need each other. They always have each other's backs, in good times and in bad, sometimes with a shared laugh or a shoulder to cry on. Their lives are forever connected, it doesn't matter how much time or space separates them, they will indelibly find each other, time after time. And when they connect or reconnect it will seem as if the space or time never happened and they pick up right where they left off. The roads of these people's lives constantly intersect and every crossing, whether deliberate or by chance is always welcomed. These people define who you are and vice versa. These are the ones you hold on too and keep close your heart and soul and you make sure they are part of your life forever. My friends are people who honestly, I would do anything for. They affect you, hopefully only for the good, if they are going the opposite way, then it may be time to remove them. Remember in this day of "likes" and social media fame, it is alright to "unfollow" people in real life. To be truly unfuckwithable, you will have to do some spring cleaning, with people in your life. You cannot change people around, but you can always change the people around you, write that done, it's going to be on the final. Maybe you don't have to remove them completely, but maybe relegate them from the "friend" title to the "acquaintance" section of your friend hierarchy. Real life is as real as it can get, I know that was not a monumental thought, but some people are so wrapped up in the digital life of theirs that they sometimes cannot fathom a reality where they mightn't be stars. 30 years ago, the internet was an escape from the real world, today the real world is an escape from the internet.

"Friendship is about finding people who are your kind of crazy" ~ unknown

Not everyone in the world is going to like you and that's ok, guess what, you aren't going to like everyone either, and that's ok too. But getting back to that quote, in a world of over 7.5 billion people, we are extremely fortunate to know that for most of us, we don't have to worry about meeting like 99.999999999% of them, but there will be a select few that we are more else tied to. Through whatever you want to believe, fate, divine intervention, or just coincidence, there will be a few that no matter the time or space between, will always find you or re-find you. Your lives will be intertwined forever. These are the people you hold onto, that are scared to you. And these are the ones you'll love, maybe platonically or maybe romantically, for the rest of your life. You won't know what they keep coming back, or you won't quite be able to explain why you two just click with each other, but you will never have to question their motives, and truth be told, they should never have to question yours either. If there comes a time when your connections end or have to end, you will feel it. It will take a physical toll on you, because you will feel you have lost a part of you, because in realty, have lost a part of you. Your friends are extensions of yourself, perhaps you see in them qualities you wish you had, so they become the parts that complete you. To capture more of the unfuckwithable vibe, maybe some of your friends should be similar to you, but maybe some should be different. Again, you are a different to person to everyone you meet, everyone will see you a different version. Its ok to be different people to different people.

"Friends buy you food. Best friends eat your food..." ~ *unknown*

True unfuckwithable friends also support you, no matter what without question, but will also give the proverbially smack to the face when you need it. They should be your biggest cheerleaders, second to yourself, to help celebrate your victories and they should be the most compassionate when you need someone to hold you up when you cannot do it on your own. In return you need to be excited and happy for them for when things go well for them. You never begrudge your friends for maybe being more successful than you, because what if the roles we reversed, you wouldn't want your friend to secretly hate you for having more. You need to be the stand-up person, bring people up when they are down, and in some cases bring them down a notch when they get a little full of themselves.

True friendships are worth more than their weight in gold, a true friendship come along only a handful of times. And when dealing with your friends, remember its quality over quantity: it always better to have 4 quarters than 100 pennies. Yes, they are the same amount, but the value is completely different. This is very visible, again, in the world of Instagram and other social media outlets. Sure, you can have 100,000 followers and be a massive influencer but how many people do you actually connect with on a deeper level, how many friends to you really have, that will be there when the On-line fame goes away, and yes it will someday. And one cannot forget that being famous on YouTube, is a lot like a 15-year-old being employee of the month at Taco Bell, in the real world it just doesn't count. Who knows where social media will take us in the future, part of me doesn't want to know?

Unfuckwithable people are their own best friend, you have to really know who you are and what you want out of this life. Your other friends, and other bonds come to you to support and push you to be the best and realest you; those who will be there no make your dreams come true and in return you come to them, to help them realizes their fullest potential. All friendships have to be two sided, it can't be on only one to carry all the weight. That can crush even the strongest person. "The Art of War" by Sun Tzu speaks about keep your friends close but your enemies closer. I've grown and discovered that if you keep your friends even closer, you don't ever have to worry about your enemies. Because your enemies won't ever get to you. Keep your circle small but keep it tight; know that it is there even when your eyes are closed.

Chapter 3

There is no telling how many miles you will have to run while chasing a dream...
If you really want to do something, you will find a way.
If you do not, you will find an excuse....

To really be unfuckwithable you must have dreams. Dreams are what keep you motivated, what make getting out of bed in the morning worthwhile. Dreams are an immensely powerful tool, they guide us into the lives that we want, sadly though the truth is it might be life we are destined to have. And to that I call bullshit. You have dreams you hold on to them and you never let anyone tell you otherwise. If your dreams do not scare you then guess what, you are not dreaming big enough. Our dreams are what will truly define our motives in life. If you dream that you want to be a millionaire, then guess what, ever decision you make is guiding you towards that dream. If you live your life without a dream, then you really aren't living at all. And an important aspect you need to understand is that you cannot just live, you have to exist and existing requires having a sense of purpose. So, when you're striving towards a goal, you are giving yourself purpose which means you are truly existing. Never forget that the meaning of life is to live a life with meaning (write that down.)

Dreams are what waking up and starting your day worth it. You must keep going, without hesitation and without complaints. Be like the Great White Shark. Does this shark complain about

Mondays? No, they are up early. Biting stuff, chasing shit, being scary – reminding everyone and everything they are a fucking shark. So, when given the choice, in a world of goldfish be the fucking shark. I just as guilty as anyone else, delaying or putting things. Hell, this book was started in my mind years ago and would start or try to start but, as I would say "life got in the way." But really, guess what, life will always get in the way, that is what life does. Things happen, for good or worse. For me one of the times life got in the way, for a great reason, was the birth of my twins. When they came into this world, I put everything on hold, or as much as I could – I had to go back to work, I had to take care of my health, I had to make sure the other lives I was responsible for were able to be taken care of as well. Everyone wears many different hats in their life, and they may sometimes interfere with your dreams and aspirations, but if you put your all into something, all of your other hats will change and shape themselves to fit what needs to be done for the dream to come to fruition.

To be unfuckwithable we are the masters of our own destiny (I know deep, right.) But our dreams and our memories shape who we are, for good or bad, and where we want to go. You cannot sit back and use your memories or your past as an excuse as to why you cannot move forward and achieve your dreams. If you cannot learn to heal from any past traumas that you may have had, then YOU are your own problem. And you will constantly be keeping blocking yourself from achieving anything worthwhile, all the while just placing the blame on the things you cannot change.

Listen everyone is messed up to a certain level, some just hide it better than others and some will always place blame on everything and everyone else rather than themselves and in some cases that person may in fact be innocent and a victim. You must take control of your life, do not ever give into your demons, no matter how strong you think they are, you are always stronger. Unfuckwithable people understand that every scar, physical or emotional, has a story behind it, so they do not judge others, but they also understand that just because you had a rough life before, it is not permission to be shitty person in the future. If you cannot take a negative and turn into a positive, you will only be blocking your own dreams and aspirations. And you will forever live a miserable life, but don't worry, misery loves company, so you'll eventually meet an equally miserable partner and you will continue the saga of misery together and more than likely pass it on to any children you may have. The last sentence was pretty harsh, I know, it was my intention, again it's not always fun hearing the truth, but if you can handle the truth, you are going to be in for a very long and sometimes painful existence.

"Excuses are lies we tell ourselves so that it doesn't have to be our fault."

-Anonymous

The old saying about excuses and assholes, everyone has one really runs true currently. There is a difference between an excuse and reason, but for a vast majority of society, they use the two terms interchangeably. A good example I hear, in the education field, "I couldn't do my homework because I had dance; my printer ran out of ink; I didn't understand it." Seriously let us dissect each excuse:

I had dance – I used this one just as an overall statement, you can change it to any activity: karate, travel soccer, scouts. Priorities have shifter drastically in recent years, and I know that can be said by ever generation regarding their relation to the next generation.

I grew up knowing school was my number one priority, but did I come home and immediately start my homework, no, I went home changed and played for a few hours. But I never complained about it, homework was done after dinner, when my parents were around and if needed, they could help me out. If I went into school the next day and didn't have it, I had no excuse and I suffered the consequence- usually just receiving a zero for the grade and in rare instances a lunch detention. Now a day's people will produce any and every "reason" why they cannot do something because they are putting things in a prioritized list that really isn't benefiting them. If you say you're going to get healthy and exercise but you don't, because maybe you had a traumatic accident and currently physically can't go to the gym, then yeah that's a reason. But eventually you will heal and get better and then what your reason. It won't exist because you'll produce another excuse, "Oh I wish I could, I just don't have the time."

Listen there are 24 usable hours in every day. If we factor in 8 hours for sleeping, that leaves up 16 hours. OK, most of us have a full-time job, that's another 8 hours, cutting our time to 8 hours remaining. If you then factor in 4 hours for family meals, bathroom time, family time, that can still leave you with 4 hours. 4 hours each week, and we will only consider Monday through Friday, that give you 20 hours a week of down time. To get healthy as the example well continue to use, you only need about an hour a day, so please save the excuse that you do not have the time. The truth is you do not want to find the time. Because you would rather talk about doing things than do them.

My printer ran out of ink: I have gotten this one quite often. I know ink is expensive, but if my car runs out of gas, I don't leave the car in the side of the road and tell my boss I cannot come to work. I go get more gas, if I can drive to the station on fumes, I do that or if I have access to a gas can I walk to a near station. Tying with this one is, I do not have a computer. Really now, in this age every single person has access to a computer. Jesus, we were conditioned by Steve Jobs to believe we needed to carry a small computer around with us. Never in the history of humankind have people had the wealth of all knowledge at the touch of their fingertips and they still do not take advantage of it.

I did not understand it: Again, internet, all the knowledge of the cosmos, simple keyboard strokes and a click of a mouse. You can YouTube any topic and teach yourself. You can learn how to play any instrument or become a day trader on the stock market. Again, if you really want to do something then you will make it happen.

Yes, you need to have your priorities in check, but how are you putting them there? What is most important should be done first, and I say "Most important" not "Most fun or easiest." You might not always like what is good for you, but occasionally maybe you need to listen to someone who has already been where you are. Just maybe, he or she has some insight and maybe they made the same mistake you are going to and they don't want to see you do that. My students always act like I myself haven't been a grade school teenager one before. No, the idea that you just had isn't original, my friends and I did/said the exact same thing 20 years ago, and you know what, it was original back then either.

When you look at the greater scheme of everything, it's always a circle, eventually everything comes back around. Maybe you might be able to alter the curve of the circle a little bit, but it's still going to be relatively the same. Make you have to make your own mark in life, and you cannot settle for just mediocre. Mediocre is average and average doesn't equate to a bank account with a lot of extra zeros attached to a larger number. Average doesn't equate to winning at life, it's not exactly the opposite, but it's not much better. Just skating through everything not owning, not winning, not living is the antithesis of what everything in this book is about.

Chapter 4

Look good, smell good, feel good

How one carries themselves says a lot to the people around you. You can walk into a store, dressed like you just woke up, hair a mess, stained dirty clothes and those employees are going to ignore you or worse, have security watch you or maybe subtlety have you leave. You look like you are not there to make the business money, then the business is not going to try to collaborate with you. On the other hand, if you dress appropriately, like you give a damn, then the workers in the stores will be more willing to assist you. Its good hygiene, showering every day, wearing nice looking clothes (nice does not translate to expensive) knowing how to use an iron and smelling good. Remember smell is the sense most associated with memory. I collect cologne; I love smell and I love to smell good. I may wear a little too much at times, funny enough I have had students tell me "Wow, Mr. Kreamer, we knew you were coming before you walked around the corner!!" Many coworkers of mine have teased me about it, but attitude is I would rather be known as the good smelling guy rather than the guy who reeks of cat-pee and sadness.

Now I know some people will immediately jump at this and say the old cliché about judging a book. Again cliché, it is not what is on the outside that matters do not really hold up anymore. Since we live in such a fake society with fake people, other opinions become fake as well. I get that there is more to an individual than his or her appearance, but in reality, how you project yourself to the world instill upon others how you see yourself, and how others need to act around you. There are biker groups, who are tattooed up and down and clad in leather and are scary looking, who protect abused kids and animals, but we do live in a judgmental society. These bikers, albeit do an amazing thing, they use the fact they are "scary" looking and are intimidating. They carry themselves in a way that dictates to the rest of the world how they wish to be treated. I've met several bikers, and upon first impression they are dudes you don't mess with, probably the most telling quality I saw on one of them was the tattoo on his neck that read "Fuck Off." I live by a rule that if an individual has a tattoo on his or her face, make sure they remain your friend. But getting back the bikers I have met. Yes, I was very intimated by them, but one you get past the tattoos (yes, I have tattoos myself) most of them are giant teddy bears. They just choose to live a certain lifestyle and look a specific manner. There is nothing wrong with that, not at all, in fact these guys usually are the epitome of being unfuckwithable. But these are choices they made, and they understand that due to their appearance, they are not likely going to be getting into any high-ranking elected spots or be a CEO of Fortune 500 company. If anything, they would scoff at the idea of wearing a shirt and tie, unless they absolutely had too.

Now not to contradict anything I may have already said, but appearance is not everything. But it is a start. It is an immediate message you send to people about how you see yourself. If you look good, hopefully you will feel good too. It drives me crazy when I hear about supermodels being so sad and depressed – you're gorgeous, the problem really comes from the fact you probably have no personality, so people get fed up with you pretty quickly. You must have beautiful heart and soul (if you believe in them) to match the beauty that on the outside. You can be a super handsome guy, but if you personality is shitty, no one will want to hang out with you, love you or be there for you, while on the flip side, you might not be uber attractive, but if your attitude reeks of positive energy and you just exude love and happiness, you'll never be alone.

You need to feel good inside and then it will billow out of you and you will look good to others. To feel good, you must take care of your own mental health – oooh touchy subject. Mental health is a real thing, there are many diagnoses and many treatments, but if you do not take care of it, it will destroy you. Now truth be told, some people do use it as a crutch, or they create their own issues – it's never an excuse to be a jerk or to not want to participate in something. If you refuse to get help, guess what, people have the right to leave you. Other people do not owe you any more patience than someone else, and even nice people have a limit to the compassion they can show. If you insist on living a life a misery, that really is your own choice, if others offer help and you refuse, that is on you, not them. You cannot blame the world for your problems if you are not actively working to fix them.

We all have our inner demons, that can affect everything we do and how the world sees us. Unfuckwithability keeps demons in check. You can never get rid of them, they are a part of you, but if they are a part of you then you have the power control them, not the other way. For some they use creative outlets, art, or music, some physical, sports or the gym, others seek therapy. The point is, do what is good for your own metal well-being and screw what anyone thinks. "You are" are enormously powerful words. When you start a sentence with these words you are making a statement about who you are, and where you are going to go. You are more than you think, always remember that – to the world you might just another random person, but to someone else, maybe even more, you might be the whole world. Live a life remembering that you just might be the reason someone else smiles each day.

"Inspire in others, the same greatness they might see in you"

Unfuckwithable people strive to make people and the world better, by not allowing others to shake their confidence. It is a state of mind that is reflected through our actions and our appearance. In a sense its understanding that the meaning of life is really to live a life with meaning. It is knowing the difference between right and wrong, an always choosing to do right, even if everyone else is choosing wrong. You are the only person who should carve your path out in this world, hopefully you choose to be the leader and not a follower; with the aspirations of reaching out and helping anyone who you see may need it. When you are gone people should miss you and when you are present, people should be excited. If the emotions are reversed, that is on you and you need to see what needs to be changed or fixed, so your "person" is something to be wanted.

You cannot judge the quality of your life by a few bad instances. Just because you had a rough patch of time, does not mean everything is lost – you can always change things, and turn your life around. The key is to never quit and take the good with the bad. Keep your head up and you eye on the prize and you would be surprised how quickly things start looking better. If you challenge yourself, let us say try to go 3 days with complaining, its amazing ow your perspective on things/life will change. When you focus only on the bad, guess what, you'll always see the bad; but if you flip that and start seeing the good, and all the opportunities you actually have, you'll see more opportunities and more good things. Nutritionists will say if you constantly eat crappy food, you are going feel and look crappy. The same can be said about energy – if you always exude

negative energy you are going to look and feel bad.

But if you radiate positives energy, you will not only

look great, but you will feel amazing.

Unfuckwithable people strive to always look and feel

good – smelling good is just a little added bonus.

Chapter 5

If your hard work does not pay off, guess what, that means you did not work hard enough

Work sucks, that's why it's called work. No one says they are going to fun, because fun isn't something you do, it's something you experience. Work has become just the opposite. I'm not saying that we have to be happy that we get to slave away and be excited little worker bees, but rather appreciate the fact that we get to go to a job or career; and the hope is that it is one that we enjoy.

The old proverb of love what you do and you'll never work a day in your life its great and all, but it's not reality. Yes, you are going to have amazing days when all the stars line up correctly and you feel it in your gut. But with every great day, there are going to come days where nothing works, everything is going wrong. Just because today was a terrible day doesn't mean that tomorrow is going to be bad as well. Tomorrow could be the greatest day because tomorrow exists in that wonderful place called "what if." There is a support group for people who don't like work, it's called EVERYONE!!!!!!...Unfuckwithable people get "it", they get "it" everywhere, in their personal and professional lives. What is "it"? It's a driving force to never settle for second best, to always want more but they know that to get more you going to have to give more. Hard work is hard, work is work, some people cannot fathom that it takes effort to succeed. Maybe you are the rare occurrence and everything you touch magically turns to gold. Maybe you were born into the right family and basically have success thrown at your face from the moment you were born. But the vast majority of us have to work and hustle, and we have to do so with a strong work ethic. And sometimes you work and you work and you sacrifice and you just don't get anywhere. That should be your cue that either you aren't working hard enough or you aren't working correctly.

This really ties back to previous chapters in regards to your dreams as well. Big dreams need to be big scares to the person who has them, but they also have to possess with them a work ethic. Most people have a full-time job of anywhere from 35-40 hours a week. Some get overtime and are compensated nicely for it. But if you really truly want to be a success, you going to have to do more.

CEOs or anyone else who wants to be unfuckwithable is definite putting in 75 to 100 hours a week, and guess what the makes them – successful, and BILLIONARES. Hard work comes with sacrifices too. You might have to forgo vacations, might have to skip out on a party or happy hour, but if you work hard now, then you can enjoy yourself. But the hustle doesn't stop just because you have a large bank account, you have to maintain it. Yes, eventually you can probably delegate more and more things, but truly unfuckwithable people will never ask someone to do something they themselves have never done before. For many years I worked as a custodial worker, I eventually moved up to manager. Guess what my employees did anything I ever asked, because I worked very hard before they worked for me. I In all honesty I have cleaned human shit off a toilet seat. I did it all, work wise, but I would never ask one of the kids who worked for me to that unless I had already done it myself. Also, as a person in a managerial position or anyplace of authority, if you want you workers to work hard, you have to show them that you are working even harder. It may not be the same type of work, and really it shouldn't be, but that isn't a reason or excuse for you to skimp on anything. Work hard and you can reap the benefits. If you don't work hard, you can get a front row ticket and watch others reap the benefits.

Work smarter, not harder is a very common cliché. Why should I break a sweat and struggle when there is an easier way?

Bill Gates, one of the rich men in the world works very intelligently, and I'm sure in his younger days he slaved away over his computer(s) developing cutting edge technology, but do you really think he still does this, no, well maybe not as much as he once did. He has thousands of employees who work for him. He paid his dues and in order for him to work smarter he had to work even smarterer (English is beautiful language). And in many instances out smart his peers as well as his competitors.

Is everyone going to billionaire, the harsh reality is no, we aren't all going to make into that tax bracket. But what everyone does have, is the chance. As mentioned above, the chance is really based on a formula of "what if" + "work ethic" + and overall desire. If you can take these elements, make it your own story, then yes you can become a success. And everyone's definition of success is different. For some, a level of success is just making ends meet. For others it looking at what your parents/guardians were able to give to you and wanting to more or to do better. And yet still others will look to Forbes Top 500, see what another half look like. They will define their success by not just how big their bank account s, but how many houses they own, how big said houses are. How many cars they own, where they travel? What you need to do is assess for yourself, what level do you want to achieve. Personally, for me, my level of success is made up of. A little bit of the levels I just mentioned. I definite want to do better than my parents. I came from a standard blue color family, and many times my dad would go to bed hungry, so his children wouldn't. I look at my accomplishments and yes, I have already achieved that level. But I still want more, you should always want more.

Greed is not always terrible thing. Is it greedy when you want to be treated well, no.? Is it greedy when you want the best for your friends and family, no? If you want something and you have worked hard to achieve, then no you aren't being greedy. Greed is just a term that some people who an envious use to bring others down, and to justify their own short comings. Envy is a disgusting emotion; learn to want what you have and you'll never be disappointed in life. Unfuckwithable people make their own success and have what they won't and will not settle for anything less.

Chapter 6

Never forget, no matter how good you are or think you are at something, there is always someone that is better than you

An unfuckwithable man or woman, knows how good they are. They also understand that then need to remain humble. The humbleness comes from remembering that there is always going to be someone who is better. maybe that person is around right now, or maybe that person has realized their ability yet, or what if, they aren't even born yet. There's a random fact I've seen on the internet for years now, I'm not even sure really how true it is, but at some point, everyone is the youngest person in the world – what, huh, how? If this is true, then everyone has a major accomplishment, they are the only one in the world, albeit for a moment or two. That's how you have to look at your talent. You might be the best basketball player in the world, or at least the greatest that the world knows about. Somewhere there's a kid practicing is layup or his turn overs and each step he or she takes on the court, is a step closer to dethroning you.

Now taking a step back to the first like: they know how good they are – lets delve into that little why don't we. If you really are good, you shouldn't have to advertise it, people should see and know and understand that you mean business and they you really are the best.

If you are constantly reminding everyone your w inner, or you so good at this and you're so good at that, WAKE UP CALL--- you aren't that great!!!

Words don't mean anything ultimately, it's your actions. If you can defend your ability by your ability then yes you are a winner and then yes you are the best. But come on, are you really great or are you just the loudest dog in park. Sometimes our silences can be the loudest voice we have, the biggest voice does not always come from biggest source.

Unfuckwithable people know they must start somewhere; they have to fail and fail and fail again. Michael Jordan, regarded as one of the all-time greatest players in the history of the NBA was cut from his high school basketball team, because he wasn't good enough, yet. He could have, pardon the pun, but taken his ball and go home. No, he took that failure as chance to get better. He practiced and practiced and eventually he become Air Jordan, and where would the world be without Space Jam. If you never know failure, you'll never know how to be a good winner. Unfuckwithability comes with the notion of being both a gracious winner but also an even more gracious loser. We can't win everything every time, it's just impossible. What we can do is learn to enjoy and embrace the small amount of time that we do win, when we can truthfully say and know the we are the best.

You must be willing to be challenged constantly. To improve you must go up against someone who is, currently, better than you. If you want to take down your competition, you must be not only as good as them, but in fact better. You need to strive to do your best without announcing it is your best. You do not need to make a "verbal" statement every time you do something. The world does not need to know your every step, remember privacy is power – people cannot ruin what they do not know. It is ok to play some cards close to your chest. The element of surprise is completely lost if you are going to announce your every move. There is a reason coaches cover their mouths when they are sending plays to their athletes. If the opposing team knows what they are going to do, then no amount of planning will be viable, your giving you enemies a copy of your playbook.

In the world of competition, winning is great, it is the most important thing. If you are really good, you never have to worry about coming in second place – and yeah second is fine for some, they'll relish in the silver medal, but don't forget that second is the first loser.

History is always written by the winners, whether you like it or not. Winners will know they might not be there forever, but history does not change. Living in America, we learn about the bravery of the colonists, how they stood up for freedom and no taxation without representation, and heroes like Washington and Franklin. We have whole books and school courses on American history, but we are only seeing our side. Do you really think the classes in England celebrate the heroism of our founding fathers, no, if anything they speak of the spoil colonists who betrayed the crown, who didn't know how good they had it? I asked a good friend of mine once, who was straight off the boat from Scotland, I asked "We learn about European history in America, did you ever learn any American?" His response struck me as weird. He said, "Yeah I think it was like a couple paragraphs in my History textbook." Unfuckwithability is a state of mind, and it is a sense of perspective. You might be a hero in your eyes and in the eyes of some people, but you might also be the villain in someone's story

Unfuckwithability comes from within, its knowing and feeling great you see yourself but also how you portray it to the world. It has not cockiness or arrogance, its confidence, and there is always an exceptionally fine line between those two sides; always know which side of the line your walking. People should respect you for your confidence, not mock or despise you for it. And once again, with confidence comes self-respect, and if you respect yourself, others will follow suit. You will never have to introduce yourself because your reputation will speak volumes for you. But that is only the start, you cannot slack or take a break. Maintaining your dignity, pride and self- respect takes work – it is incredibly easy to slip down the rungs of the ladder, but difficult to climb back up. For me, once I stop respecting you, its damn near impossible for me start again. It is much like trust with me. Once you betray my trust, I may forgive, but I never forget, and you will never regain my trust.

Now to maintain a healthy level of humbleness, a person should learn to help others, even when nobody is willing to help you. If you put yourself out there and do the right thing, eventually people will see and understand that you are a force to be reckoned with. But a truly unfuckwithable person will always do the right thing, even when no one is watching; that is the true sign of good character. Help someone who has no conceivable way of returning the favor, because karma may work slow, but it always comes back to you.

Chapter 7

If you are the smartest person in the room, you are in the wrong room.

This chapter does coincide with the general theme of other chapters. Knowing your limitations and abilities, and an overall desire to strive for better. If you are the smartest person you know, there's a problem – who can you learn from, because obviously you know everything and no other person possible teach you anything. We build ourselves from those around us. Much like being the smartest, if your nicest person you know that means everyone else is not, so why do you surround yourself with people who cannot possibly bring you up. If your company cannot improve who you are, it can only ruin it. Do not let others bring you down, inspire them and bring them up.

An effective intelligent person never allows her or his emotions to control them. Have you ever watched a debate and one of the participants gets heated and starts rambling, it is sad? Watch any political rally where people are so enthusiastic about their belief that they cannot bear to listen to anyone who remotely disagrees with them. A Common phrase currently is "Facts don't care about your feelings" and this cannot be any truer. Facts are facts, unless proven differently, they are accepted as the truth as well. Emotions change, sometimes they can change on the drop of hat. You should never allow you emotions to get the better of you. It's been said you should never go to the supermarket when you're hungry, your hunger will control what you buy and you may get things you don't want, shouldn't eat or can't afford. The same can be said when having a conversation. Do not get into a debate when you are angry. I don't like to fight and I have been very guilty of letting my emotions get the better of me; in my younger and dumber years when I would have a verbal argument with someone, I immediately went for the jugular. I would say the worst things imaginable; I would attack that persons most vulnerable points. Sure, it is an effective way to win a fight, but sadly you cannot ever *unsay* those things. Even when tempers come down and cooler heads prevail, those words will still have been spoken. And no matter how any time you try to apologize or make amends, that person will have the image of you saying those vile things in the head forever.

"The axe always forgets, but the tree always remembers," ~ Unknown

Do you want to be known that way in someone's mind, if you a rational or sane person the answer is no. So, to keep with the unfuckwithable aspect I am trying to implore upon you, unfuckwithable people can keep their emotions in check.

Unfuckwithable people do have feelings, we have emotions – emotions are not bad, and they are not a sign of weakness – please stop with any thinking like that. Its ok to get mad, its ok to be happy and it is ok to be sad – wat you do with these emotions is what really matters. Anger is fine, rage is bad. Sad is ok, depressed is bad. You must give yourself check occasionally too. If you find you are constantly flipping out and raging over stupid shit, then you need to seek help, just like if you are constantly s depressed, please get help. Everyone gets down, sometimes for good reason, other times its unexplainable. I suffer from depression, it sucks. There have been many times I wake up and I do not want to get out of bed at all, I want to cover my head and escape. I feel I have been able to control the monster, no matter how much I don't want to get up, I tell myself "to get up and out the big boy pants on, people depend on you." I still get spells, don't get me wrong, but I find for me personally the gym helps out a lot, but more than that my kids are what get me through the rough patches. I look at them and want so much for them, I want them to be the smartest and best – I mean not to sound biased or anything, but they already are. They are my masterpieces, my Mona Lisa, my Sergeant Pepper, my Citizen Kane, they are the ones that inspire me to be completely unfuckwithable – and yes, I won't let them read this until they are much older, recently I have tried to curb my language around them. Sometimes I wish my dad did that for me, the first words in Italian I ever learn were curse words, and it wasn't until much later after my dad passed away that my mom finally broke the news to me that my dad couldn't speak a word of Italian – so really I don't what words he said when he got frustrated with a project.

"I don't need anger management; I just need you to stop making me angry!!!!" ~ unknown

Frustration is often confused with anger, but they are quite different. The one thread that ties them together is that frustration often leads anger. If you are constantly angry about everything or nothing, you need an outlet, a hobby or something. Unfuckwithable people are willing to change, so you must assess what is going on in your life and you may have to make some changes. Nothing changes nothing, change changes everything. Unfuckwithability cannot be confused with unbreakable or unwavering, because the latter two terms relate to the idea of not adapting. You must be able to adapt; evolve if you dare. Look at who you are right now, in this moment; now look at who you were 10-15 years ago. More than likely you may have some similarities, but you should be different.

Life experiences, for good or bad change us and shape who we are, and ultimately, it's the best version of ourselves for this very moment – if it was the absolute best, then we wouldn't have this moment. Now think of where you will be in 10-15 years. Who knows what tomorrow will bring, but whether you are a part of it or not, tomorrow is going to happen? And you cannot hold on the anger – every minute of anger is a minute you could have been happy. Just because today was an awful day does not mean that tomorrow will be as well; tomorrow has the possibility of being the greatest day ever.

Solving everyone's problem isn't your job in life. But when you are presented with an issue, remind yourself of this little phrase – if you aren't part of the solution, then you are part of the problem. How you look at the problem is also a reflection of your part in it. We can see problems as obstacles, which of course they are, but when we start to see them as an opportunity, that is when you are unfuckwithability grows. How can this issue or problem be solved and how can this make me a stronger, better person? Ask yourself what would the best version of you do in these situations. Do you back down and let the problem dictate the outcome, or do you attack it like a fat kid after a cupcake (calm down, I was a fat kid once too). You need to show the problem and the world you're in charge. You don't have to be an 'alpha-male/female' to be a person to be wrecked with, just a person with the confidence and self-respect to not take shit from anyone or anything. You make your own luck, but remember if you're good or smart enough, you'll never have to rely on luck (write that down, its important.)

You can maintain being a nice person, but as mentioned before in this book, niceness isn't permission to be a door mat. You cannot allow the world or the people around you to use you and treat you like crap. Because how you see yourself will reflect with how the world sees you. If you want to the world to know you are a bad ass unfuckwithable guy or girl, then you have to establish in your mind how bad ass you really are. How you think will manifest its way to how you are seen. Your confidence will boost, you will have an air about yourself, and your presence will be known. It cannot happen overnight, it takes time and reprogramming how you think. There are plenty of other books and products out there that can help you re train your brain, but the first step has to come from within, you have to accept the fact that you need to be "rebuilt" – make you better and stronger, emotionally and physically. Someday, you'll look back and wish you had done it sooner, because life is a lot better when you make life live for you instead of you living for life.

Chapter 8

You catch more flies with honey than with vinegar....
But not every fly should be caught, do not be afraid to
swat the ones that should not get to close

An unfuckwithable person is a nice person and life winners aren't always cut throat. Don't let these terms make you think you have to be cold heart jerk – don't get me wrong, there's always a time and a place for being cold hearted, but it's not supposed to be a permanent fixture I your life. Be nice, people will like you a hell of lot more, and although being liked isn't the most important thing in the world, it is important if you want any level of success. If you are good to others, guess what, in most cases they will be good to you. If you are nothing but a dick to others, do not be surprised when you have nobody by your side. I don't ever treat anyone poorly, what I do I treat them accordingly – meaning, what they give is exactly what they get. So, if you are good to me, I will be good to you.

But it is ok to keep some at a distance. You do not necessarily have to be nice to every single human being you encounter. Some people will just irk you; you won't know why and maybe you'll try and give them a second or third chance, but no matter what, you just can't bring yourself to liking them. And that is ok. And then occasionally someone may try too hard to get into your inner circle, its ok if they aren't a good fit, and those are the ones you need to keep at a distance. Nice people can be rude when the time calls for it. And it's a sad truth, but sometimes you just have to accept some people are just real shitty and that there really isn't any good in them, and they aren't worth your time or effort. They cannot and will not change, so you need to edit them out of your universe.

Do not be the person, who is so utterly clueless, they don't know how to read people. Be the guy or girl that when you are around, people are happier. Be the light in the world of dark. Because if you are total jerk and people do not want you around, guess what, you will be a lonely person. And another key point to remember is this: If your presence makes no difference to someone, then neither will your absence. People should miss you when you are not around. They should not feel a sense of relief or even happy when you are not around. If you won a free tropical vacation, then yes, your friends should be happy you are on a vacation, not that you are not around though.

Making sure others know that you are nice person is terrific, but they must also know it is not an invitation to walk all over you. Nice people can say no, that is acceptable. Kindness is a quality that should never be taken for granted by anyone. Everyone has her or his limits though. Even the nicest person can be pushed to the point that they can become quite a scary individual when they have had enough. It is never good to get someone to go to that place, but it is even more important to not allow others to get YOU to that point.

When you treat people like crap, they will not respect you. If they do not respect you, they will not listen to you. If they will not listen to you, then you will have even more work ahead of you, because you will be going at it alone.

Some people believe in using fear, while others believe in using love to keep loyalty. You must surround yourself with loyal people – loyalty is worth 100X its own weight in gold. But the how to attain loyalty without having to use fear as a motivation tool? The answer is simple, you have to demonstrate yourself the qualities you are looking for in others. You have to show your loyalty to others and in turn they will show theirs to you. I am loyal to a fault, this was touched on in previous chapters as well, so if you think you've read this before, yeah you probably have. My people are my people and for those individuals I am willing to do anything for. My friends know that I'm the type of friend who will help them hide a body, but if they ever cross me or are disloyal, they know I'm the kind of guy who knows HOW to hide a body. Obviously, the body is a metaphor, or is it? A good friend is that person who will come bail you out of jail, but a great friend, a loyal friend will be sitting right next to you in the jail cell saying "I can't believe we did that shit" hopefully laughing. And again, I'm not encouraging you to do anything stupid, but rather enjoy your friends and the time you have with them, because unlike just about every commodity we have, the one that cannot be refilled is time. Time is a fleeting thing, and we must make the moist of the limited amount we are given. It was mentioned in a previous chapter about living a life worth talking about, but there was a phrase "YOLO" that was pretty popular several years ago, and I couldn't stand it. It stands for "you only live once' and idiots used it as an excuse to go out and do stupid random things, that could get them hurt or worse. When you really think about it, you don't really live only once – you die only once, but you can live every day. The mantra of YOLO really should be interpreted as "you are given only one life; you need to make the most of it; you need to live a life worth living. You should do something that matters with your life, even if it's something small: helping at a soup kitchen, rescuing a puppy from the shelter, and being a mentor to someone. Then you can say your life had a purpose. The meaning of owning life really boils down to owning a life with meaning, owning a life worth living.

There is a wonderful poem called "The Dash" by Linda Ellis, that sums up what the meaning of life should be. Basically, the premise of the poem is that there are two important dates in every one's life, they define the start and end of our lives, but everything else we do, no matter how big or small, is defined by a little dash (-). Life is so much more than this little mark. The lives we effect, the lives create, the mark you make on everything around you. Your legacy must mean something.

"Be so great, that you can't be ignored..."

Everything does come to end, and more than likely we will not know it is the end until we look back. There was a time when your mom or dad held you and then put you do not for the very last time. There was a time when you and your friends played outside for the last time, and you did not realize it was to be the last time. For a little more of a modern flair, there will be a last group chat. When the moment passes by, all we have left are memories and, in some instances, unanswerable questions. We don't really understand how important these moments are, until with think back and remember them. It would be amazing if we could have a little foresight and know we were living in the "good old days" before they become just the "good old days."

When your gone, your gone for good, the only thing left will be the memories of you in the minds of the people you leave behind. An unfortunate fact though is eventually the time will come that someone will visit your grave, for the last time. Your headstone will still stand, and someone passing through the cemetery will stop and read it, but eventually you will fade into obscurity. It only takes about a generation or so before you are forgotten – be honest, how many times have you visited your great great grandparents' graves – or do you even know who they were?

What can you do to prevent being lost to the annals of time? What we do in life matters. How we treat others matters. We will not be defined by our possessions, but by the lives we affect, whether for good or bad. An unfuckwithable person will leave the world and people in it, better than had they never existed. Their absence will not only instill a longing for them, but pride in the those they knew, because those who they knew, know they are forever changed by being their world.

But the point of the chapter went a little off topic, so to recap, do not be jerk unless you are left with no other choice. I often remind my students they should not be a jerk to me, because that will force me to be a jerk back them. And I am a whole lot better at being a jerk to them, than they are to me. I'm constantly reminding my students that no teacher enjoys yelling at their students. I don't wake up in the morning and think "how can I make a day miserable or a student?" Guess what teachers do take things home, emotional baggage. I cannot tell you how many times I was up late worried about my students, because as an educator we do become surrogate parents, uncles/aunts, or older siblings – whether we want it or not. Our students will not remember much about what we taught them, rather they will remember more about how they were treated or what was said to them. I have been guilty of saying mean things out of anger, and sadly that is what those kids take away from their time in my class. But I have also been awarded for my dedication and my open heart with my students. I have a stack of letters from students telling me I was their favorite teacher; I have also written letters on behalf of students for colleges and employers. My room is decorated with shirts and banners from the college or career paths my formers students have followed after they've graduated. I have been honored by being selected to speak on behalf a student at scholarship dinners, which was by invite, by the student. I have been present at sweet 16's in which I was given the chance to light a candle with the guest of honor during that ceremony. I have been extremely lucky to have been the officiant at several former student weddings. There have not always been happy moments I got to share; I have lost too many students due to uncontrollable circumstances either by their own admission or not. I've been to funerals, where my students are burying siblings. One instance, my student (who in my entire career, I will forever called my school little sister, because I was much younger, so my rapport with her was more big brother-ish) was holding herself together at her older brothers funeral, and then when I was in front of her on the receiving line, she finally lost it and fell into me sobbing. She later told me that as soon as she saw me, she felt safer and was able to feel the grief she was experiencing. I got to have these moments and experiences because these students had a positive memory of his or her time in my class. But also, because I was fair and treated them well, and because they could always tell I cared, and for those reasons I was a winner in their life. Ask yourself if you've ever had these moments or experiences. Have you made an impact on someone, positive ones should be your focus? Are the people around you better because of you and are you better because of the people around you? You need to make sure the answer to both of those questions is a rousing YES!!!!

I've have had thousands of students, and there are some who will say I was awful and unfair, and they hated me – you cannot be a god to everyone. Remember what I said before, you aren't going to be the same person to everyone. People will base their perspective of you on how they perceive the world. If they look at the world like a hell hole, then it will be very difficult for them to see you in a positive light. And sometimes some personalities just don't click, and just because you don't get along with or like someone, doesn't mean you cannot be cordial with them. You will have to coexist with people you don't like, that's part of life.

<u>Chapter 9</u>

In life, some days you are the bug, and some days you are the windshield.

Not every day is going to be the greatest. If all we ever had we great days we'd never know what a great day is, because we have to have something to compare it to. The bad times help us to remember how great the good times really are. It comes down to balance – we have to take learn to handle the bad just as well as you can handle the good. If you can master that, you can master anything. We all have a difficult day, sometimes it leads to bad spell that can last for a little while. No matter that we do, however positive we try to be, everything just comes up wrong. You feel like you are in a rut and the end is nowhere in sight. What would an unfuckwithable person do in this situation? Part of being unfuckwithable is understanding that you cannot control everything in the world. Yes, bad things will happen to you, that is a fact. You'll ask why, since in your mind you've been nothing but good person. You'll ask, god, the universe, who or whatever you choose to believe in why, and maybe you'll get an answer, but maybe you won't. You can either dwell on it and let it control your behavior or you can accept it, learn from it, and move on. Yes, terrible things suck, that is why they called bad. And you will ask why it happened to you or what could you have done to prevent it. Either way you cannot undo it. But again, hopefully you can use it as a learning experience. You cannot let the wight of the past crush your present and destroy your future (write that down). You got to always keep your head up. Just because today was a shitty day, does not mean tomorrow is going to be. Tomorrow, still, and always will, have the potential to be amazing. It is up to you. If you sit back and do not change anything, nothing will change, and you will have no other person to blame but you.

"Being around people reminds me of how much I love being by myself..." ~ *unknown*

When we mess up, most of the time its due to our own accord, and if it is not it is still because of choices we made. Sometimes it is the choice we made to hang out with the wrong person. Time along gives you plenty of time to reflect on things. Do not be afraid to do things alone. If you failed, at least you tried; if you succeed, you do not have to share the credit with anyone. I learned this lesson in my college years. I could have stayed local and gone to college close home, but I knew I wanted to get away from family. Not because I had to get a way, I needed to. I ended up going 500 miles away, not a huge distance, I did not have to travel across the country, just the state. At college I had friends who lived 15 minutes away, they went home every day or every weekend. I could not do that; I was stuck waiting for vacations and holidays to go home. It taught me how to be self-reliant. Weekends were sometimes lonely because everyone would go home. I had to learn to fend for myself- laundry and groceries, all things that as a teen you take for granted.

This helped me later when I had an apartment, which meant I had to worry about rent, and everything that goes into maintaining a "home". I also learned that I can be alone without being lonely – there is a difference. When I was alone, I loved it, I could come and go as I pleased, I could do whatever I wanted whenever I wanted to do it, it was my first inclination of being unfuckwithable –

because I had to answer to no one other than myself. I learned to love "my time" and it helped me to really figure out who I am, or at the time, who I was, because this was 20 plus years ago and many different lives ago. Even to this day I love alone time, although life has changed drastically for me, becoming a father of twins – who are the two greatest things to ever happen to me. But "my time" has diminished a lot, I am usually relegated to when they go down for a nap which gives me sometimes an hour or so where I can focus on myself. I do believe in taking care of yourself first. That's not me saying my kids or other aspects of my life are not important, but if you cannot take care of yourself, how the hell can you take care of someone else. It reminds of, again in a different life, when I was a volunteer firefighter, the first lesson I was taught in the academy was "In a burning building, you are your number one priority, because if you can't save yourself, you aren't able to save someone else."

Really think about that. If you do not know who you are, how can anyone else know you. Being alone allows you to sort out the important stuff and the bullshit in the world. And after a while, you really started not worrying about the mundane stupidity of everyday life. Then there would be times I would be lonely; just missing any kind of connection with another person-friendship or romantic. You want to have those ties with others, especially the ones you have deemed to be incredibly important to you and your life. Making those kinds of connections are key to not just being unfuckwithable, but for your overall mental well-being. And as mentioned in other chapter, you have to take care of yourself emotionally, because you have to keep your emotions in check, so they don't over power you and cloud your ability to think and make decisions.

"If it doesn't add to your life, it doesn't belong in your life" ~ *unknown*

Unfuckwithability can coincide with simplicity, keeping your life simple and drama free is a pillar to this lifestyle and philosophy. Life is so much better when there is no drama. In my experience, most issues or drama come from people who claim they don't like drama, that's the definition of irony. Honestly if you have drama in your life, you really need to take a step back and reevaluate what is going on in your life. If you're the cause of it, then you should seek some kind of help; if it's the company you keep that is the root, then you need to remove them from your life. Again, in this day of social media, it is ok to unfollow/unfriend people in real life (write that down, its important). Unfuckwithable people know how to declutter their emotions and their lives. If you aren't making me a better individual then you can see your way to the door. If you find it hard to let people go, because you might really care about them, maybe help them seek help. Or at least call them out on their toxic behavior. And yes, overly dramatic people are toxic, because even though they may not intentionally do it, they will suck the life out of the people around them, and spread their negativity like the plague. Negativity is a disease, and there is only one cure for it, positivity, but there's no one source for it – it'll be different for everyone. People will find their positive energy pursuing their passion, spending time at the beach, playing with a puppy, who knows. But as an unfuckwithable person, find your passion, find a hobby, find something that's gets you to enjoy your life. When you spend your time enjoying the things around you, then you won't have time to be a "Debbie-downer." But as I mentioned earlier, life cannot always be rainbows and butterflies. Bad events will occur beyond your control – will you make them worse or will you try to make things better, that is your choice.

"Everything happens for a reason, but sometimes that reason is you're stupid and you made a bad choice"

You always have a choice. Once you reach a certain age, really the sooner the better, your decisions are your choices, no one can make them for you or really what I should say is no one should be making them for you. There are exceptions, a small child should not be given the choice to stick a fork in an outlet or not, that is where a parent or adult has to step in. But once that child reaches a maturity level, their choices are their own. Sometimes we good choices and sometimes we make bad ones – both are ok, because we are humans. Everything happens for a reason, but occasionally the reason bad things happen is because your stupid and you did something stupid. Are you going to own it or blame someone else? A person who cannot or will not take responsibility for their own actions is a toxic person. Very rarely are things completely out of your control, if you are the one making the choices, you have the control. Sometime you will be faced with the lesser of two evils, and the you won't like either choice, but you may still have to choose. The best thing you can do in this situation is to make a choice and stand by it. Do that every time you have to choose. Own it and don't let anyone sway you or change your mind, just because it's the choice they don't agree with. Making choices is a guarantee that you will not always be the most popular person, and when you become unfuckwithable, you won't care who likes you or who doesn't, that's a true sense of freedom. And when you have a sense of freedom, then you have reached the pinnacle, you are a winner and you have won at this game called life.

Chapter 10

Sucking at something is the first step towards being good at it

When you care deeply about something, that is a mark that you have won at life and that you are unfuckwithable. In life you have to have a hobby, something you enjoy doing, that doesn't become a nuisance to you or work. It can be anything you want, whether you take up gardening, lifting weights, anything that gets you out of your mundane routine of wake up, go to work, come home and go to bed. Hobbies can give you a purpose; if you have no purpose, then why bother getting out of your bed in the morning. The purpose has to go beyond your obvious responsibilities. Of course, in the world, you need to go to work, unless you are very fortunate and have a great trust fund or rich spouse.

But to be good at something you have to start, and when you start you are going to be horribly bad at it. Remember even the mightiest oak tree started as a tiny acorn. When you step out of your comfort zone, you'd be surprised what you might be able to do, because in the end you are only competition and your only road block. Again, the theme of being your own hero comes back into play here. Your own hero, what does that really mean – it means be the person who you think can do the impossible. You're probably the reason for your own pit falls – you're probably you're biggest critic (and that you should be); you have probably labeled your own limitations, and yes you should know what they are, but you should also be the one who tears them down. Being afraid to try something new is a good feeling, it's the first sign that you are doing something new and that you are out of your comfort zone. You might just surprise yourself if you take a little initiative and motivation and do the new experience and have that once in a life time moment of no fear. But you have to be the one who does it, not for anyone else, do it for yourself. You want to win at life, sometimes it requires you to grab life by the proverbial balls.

Is every experience or everything you try going to work out, no that would be a grossly impossible feat. But you know what, who cares – did it cause you or anyone around any harm, then really the failure doesn't matter. What matters is that you tried. Unfuckwithable people are not afraid to try, they aren't scared to take a blind step. If you can walk away from it unscathed, physically or emotionally, then even if you lost you still won. Winners are the most important part of any competition – sorry to the losers who really gave it their all, and really put their heart and soul into it. History doesn't remember those people; it remembers and celebrates the winner. But winners can constantly change, right now we have Facebook, which has cleared established itself and a main stay in the world of social media and technology. But who remembers Myspace – Tom was everyone's friend? But let's go further, what happened to Friendster – some of you might be getting a blast of reminiscing emotions and others are going to be baffled by these names. Zuckerberg won, for right now, because who knows what might come next. Yes, the others two thought they won, but they have long since gone the way of triceratops and pterodactyl. But is there something slowly evolving now that will replace Facebook or has its hold onto society gotten so strong that it won't allow itself to pushed aside. Are you willing to let society push you to the side, just because you tried and fail at something? You have to fail, and you have to fail often. That is when you'll learn to learn from your mistakes and how you can grow as a person. If you stay in the same place, mentally, then everything you do will always have the same outcome. You have to be willing to change your mindset and think like a winner. You do that enough and you will become a winner. If you think of yourself as unfuckwithable, eventually you will become unfuckwithable. And of course, you will have detractors, people who will criticize you and may even hate you. For the ones that hate you, I say, let them hate. You've had some kind of effect on them, and more than likely it stems from a sense of jealousy. They see themselves as some who cannot be unfuckwithable, and the only way they can feel good about their short comings is to break your accomplishments down. Those people don't matter, so they don't need to exist in your

"Excuse me, you're blocking my path to success!!!"

We are always standing on the shoulders of the giants that came before us. We are always making things "new and improved" – well if they are new, how can they be improved, isn't that the point of being new. Always strive to pick one of those two for yourself, either improve yourself or try to make yourself brand new. You may find inspiration in someone else's work of effort, but don't let that be the basis for your life – establish you're own routine, look at what they did and if it worked for them, try it for yourself, and if it does work, ten make it your own. Don't do exactly what they did, you're living your own life, not replaying someone else's. Write your auto-biography, don't let someone else tell the story of who you are, notice I said who you are, not who you were. Because although you don't want to live someone else's life, it's a kind of a good feeling when you know you've inspired others, and maybe after your days have ended, someone

113

wants to tell story of who you were. It's a way to be remembered through the time after you have passed away, and hopefully there is someone who wasn't even alive at the same time as you, who will learn about you and follow how you lived your life and they will take what you did, learn from you example, see your successes and your failures, and apply it to their life and make it their own; continuing a cycle of admirations and inspiration. Allowing you to become the giant whose shoulders they are standing upon.

People always love to try new things just as long as they are the exact same as the old things. You can always seek out help from others. Asking for help is not an omission of weakness; strong people can look to other strong people for assistance. Now this is not about therapy or mental health, that was covered in other chapters, this is about actually needing help to attain a goal. You might not like someone's technique(s) but if they work for that person, who is to say that it cannot work for you either. You cannot be so set in your ways that you refuse to see things differently. If you want to win at life, then you need to adapt; you may have to switch things up, because if the old ways weren't working, then you're inviting yourself to stay the same. Now evolution does not always reward the strongest, but as an individual you can choose what you improve on. You might only need a little tweaking here and there; well those minor changes now could translate to a huge transformation later. Never settle for less than what you deserve, because if you do then you are going to get less than what you deserve.

As mentioned before, you need to be your own hero, but that doesn't mean you can't also look up to others – just don't ever put someone on a pedestal who doesn't deserve it. When you put someone high up, that just means they have a longer way to fall and a harder climb back up. It is not fair to them or to yourself, because you may just set yourself up for major disappointments. To be unfuckwithable, appreciate those around you, their abilities, and their imperfections. We all are only as good as our imperfection lead us. No one is perfect so to expect them to be is an impossible and unfair challenge. Take everything in this book; I have not been able to master everything all at the same time. When I improve in area, I may stumble in another, and that is ok. Unfuckwithability comes with a sense of understanding that you cannot do everything, and you cannot be everything to everyone. That is way too much pressure to put on yourself. Learn to delegate and choose what is most important and what can wait; priorities are important – establish what is going to be beneficial and accomplish that first. Sort things out and then you can assess the value them as much as the value of your own time.

Chapter 11

Be real, there is nothing more real than being real

You are your own person, you shouldn't try to be just like anyone else, and you shouldn't change who you are, unless obviously you have identified some toxic behaviors, then by all means change. But at the root of your personality, you must stay true. It's better to for the people to hate you for being true to yourself than having everyone love you for being something you aren't. Could you honestly look at yourself in the mirror every day and be happy knowing you are living a lie? I hope not. An ugly truth will always be better than a beautiful lie. Let that sink in, and then self-evaluate – is the life you're living currently the truest form of who you are or are you lying to yourself and to the world around you. If you need an animal analogy to help you see this: It's better to be a lonely lion than a popular sheep.

Stand up for what you believe, its might not be a popular belief but hold on to it. Don't let people sway you and make you feel bad for having an opinion. And no person should have the power over you to dictate what you should feel or think. Be strong in your convictions but be compassionate to be open to hearing others people's thoughts and feelings. If you ever find yourself in a situation where emotions are starting to cloud either your intelligence or actions, or hose of someone else, just remain silent. Sometimes our silence can be our loudest voice. Silence isn't a sign of weakness either.

People in control don't have plan big moves out loud for everyone to see and hear.

Emotion is a very powerful tool. Look at public speakers- one technique that has been taught for centuries is how to evoke an emotional response from your audience. Yes, emotions are a very good thing, but they can also be a hindrance in a way. Emotion has a tendency of getting intertwined with opinion; "I feel" and "I think" are completely different ways to start a conversation or monologue. One is tied to emotion whereas the latter is an opinion. When both of these are set aside, you are left with facts. The beautiful thing about facts, is they don't care about who is right or wrong, and they certainly don't care how "you" feel. Unless proven otherwise facts don't change often. Facts are real, you cannot get around that and you should celebrate them. Model yourself after facts; only change yourself if it's been proven or understood that something needs changing, i.e. any toxic behaviors.

Being real and truthful might not make you the most popular person, but "truth" be told, winning at life involves more than being the most beloved person. You might actually be hated and you might have to fight for your beliefs; are your beliefs worth those sacrifices. To some people they will be an astounding yes, others may waiver on the answer. You must be firm in you believes, not rigid. The difference being firm is strong but bendable, rigid is unmoving. You cannot live your life wearing blinders and seeing only what you want to see. You must be open to new ideas and different opinions. If you surround yourself with people who only agree with you, you cannot grow as person. Don't have "yes men" and don't ever let yourself become a "yes man." Surround yourself with people who are going to challenge you, they will force you to level up and become a better you.

Do something, stand for something and more than anything BE SOMETHING!!! The worst people are those who are all talk – there is a big difference between thinking and actually doing. Talking can get things rolling, but working is what build empires. Ultimately you really are always only one decision away from a totally different life. That decision could lead in a positive way, but it could also lead to a negative. Choosing to invest in the latest IPO could make you incredibly rich, if the stock takes off. But what if you invest and the stock tanks, you could go bankrupt. Make your decisions wisely, be rational, be factual – follow your brain first, then let your heart bring up the rear.

It's the biggest joke ever played on the human race, having two types of thinking, that mostly work in opposing directions. You have your brain and you have your heart. When dealing with situations which side do you listen to? Everything written here so far has answered that with: your brain – it's the facts that matter. But an unfuckwithable person cannot be a cold machine, you need to use your heart. But your heart and brain have to work in harmony with each other, not against. If you can harness both and have them unified, you will always win at life.

The idea of romance, not the lovey candle lit dinner and sonnets part, but the idea of genuine love and care does play an integral part in winning in life, because you have to have a love affair with life. To win at something you have to love it, you have to have passion. Maybe you love cars. You don't like cars, you love them, everything about the mechanical and technical aspects, and you want to build your own. This will become a labor of love; you're doing it because you feel some sort of accomplishment whenever you make a significant step towards its completion. And when your car is finished, and you start the ignition, it's yours, you know everything about it – it's become your baby. Nobody can, or should, take that away from you and now you have the chance to share your knowledge and share you experience with others. This is what real winning looks like, getting others excited or interested in something you do and sharing it with them.

Following your gut isn't just an expression, we do have a biological inner voice that guides us. Call it your conscience or divine intervention or whatever, but you have to train yourself to follow it. It's your own personal moral compass – as a rational human, you know the difference between right and wrong, and you know which path you want to go down. But just because it's what you want, your gut might say otherwise. What you want and what you need are sometimes vastly different things. Ultimately you will always get to where you need to be, just the path might not be a quick one, there may be a ton of detours. There is no short cut to life, it's a journey not a destination, so you need to enjoy the ride. Enjoying the ride gives you freedom, and freedom breeds unfuckwithability. Hindsight is always 20/20, its always easier to look back and wish you had made different choices, and the worst feeling is when you say to yourself "I wish I had listened to my gut." It takes work, because again, you have your brain and your heart battling, now we throw in your gut, and the gut doesn't play loyal to either of the other two. Sometimes it will agree with your brain, and then sometimes it'll side with your heart. Its unpredictable so you can never really figure out which side will.

A real person will always be able to make their own sunshine. Yes, it is another one of those cliché ideas, but when you look at it, it is true. When you are real, you don't sugar coat things, and you don't need others to do that for you either. You can see situation for what it really is, and you can choose to make it better. When you make that choice, it is what you gut is saying to do, then you are winning. You cannot control everything, but for the few thigs you can, always try to make them better. Better does not mean it is all rainbows and puppies playing in a field. Better means not letting the dark or the negative have any sort of influence over you. You choose to let the dark in, sometimes it knocks gentle, other times it appears as if its banging on your door so hard, the door starts to splinter. Opening the door and letting it in means you have lost and your letting something else control you. Unfuckwithable winners don't let shit control them. Real people can let the shit roll off their shoulders. You don't have to hang onto every bad thing that has ever happened to you – if you do, you're going to be very unhappy for the rest of your life. Let go. It's a simple to sentence phrase. But it is difficult for so many people, they cling on to it, because for those individuals, they define their happiness by their misery, no matter what happens to them, some people in this world will only ever be happy when they're miserable – they fall into the category of toxic people, and you need to remove them from your life, as quickly as possible. Real winners define their happiness by their happiness. Winners do not always have to win, but they take everything, good or bad, and they make it work for them – they own the world in a regard. And the world is owned by winners, but it is watched by losers. Don't be the sideline hero, the guy who "could have" done more, but chose not to. Real people go for it – sometimes the win, sometimes they fail, but every time they learn. The more you learn the stronger and more real you get to become. When you develop, you are sense/feeling of strength make sure no one can take that from you. Unfuckwithable people do not let others rattle them, they can take the worst that the world or the people around them can dish out and let it roll off their shoulders.

Chapter 12

Do not over complicate things, keep it simple

There's a great line of DYI books that follow the K.I.S.S. method, Keep It Simple, Stupid. Our society has a real problem with making things for more complicated than they really need to be. We over think, over analyze and over compensate practically everything. What we really need to do is to slow down and stop thinking once in a while. Life doesn't have to be as hard as we make it. Sometimes the best solution or best escape is to go outside on a sunny day and roll in the grass or play with a dog. If you want to really understand what it means to win at life, you have to know that no matter what is going down in the world, tomorrow is going to happen. Tomorrow has been happening, on this planet, for something like 5 billion years, so when we put that into perspective, does what we really do here and now make a difference. In the grand scheme, no it doesn't, but hopefully on a smaller scale we have a positive impact on those around us. And to win this game we call life, you have to leave every situation and every encounter with someone, being better than before.

Now there are obvious reasons to get worked up over things – bills, health, the safety of your loved ones etc., but at the same time an unfuckwithable person isn't easily shaken. With these issues that can occur, keep a clear mind – again the idea of using your brain and thinking logically comes into play. Don't get some worked up that your emotions start to get the better of you. When your emotions start clouding your judgement, that's when your work will get sloppy and you might end up making things either worse or you may create problems that didn't exist before.

Now living a simple life, doesn't mean you have to give up any dreams of being a billionaire, you don't have to live in a tiny house and grow your own food and make your own clothes. What this philosophy really means is to weed out what isn't important and just focus on what is. And what is important to one person may not be important to someone else. You'd think certain things would be universal, health, financial stability, family – but to each their own. People do not always put the same priorities in the same order. For some play is far more important than work, and if that works for them, then they are winning. If you live your life where you work hard now so you play later and you find that works for you, then guess you are winning too. Take out the stuff that you won't care about in five years, but in order to that you have to look beyond the here and now. But in order to live simply, you have to start. Throwing stuff out I find is the first step. Any emotional baggage you may be carrying around with you, just let it go – I know easier said than done, but for you own well-being you have to learn to let go. The past is the past and you can leave it there. There's no reason why your past needs to dictate your present or control your future.

Declutter would be the next step – work with physical possessions. Maybe it's time to clean out your closet, or get rid of those CD's you don't listen to anymore (I fear some of my readers may ask "what's a CD?"), get a dumpster and clean out our basement and garage. We collect or gather so much crap that we will never actually use or ever need again. If it's taking up space but is useless, get rid of it. For the closet idea, I started doing the hanger trick several years ago. The hanger trick, on January 1st or whenever you want to start, reverse all your hangers so they come over the bar from the back. Anytime you wear something and put it back into your closet put it the normal way. After a year anything that is still reversed means it hasn't been used or worn in a year and probably won't be ever again. Take these items out and donate them somewhere. You don't have to judge others and be judged about your possessions – if you do, you are losing and I feel bad for you. If you are constantly judging yourself by what you have or more importantly what you don't have, you are always going to be disappointed. Don't confuse disappointment with not be satisfied. Not being satisfied means you want more, and it's a good thing to want more out of life, out of everything you do. It's what gives you motivations to strive and to work harder. Disappointments will just lead to anger and resentments and bitterness. Ultimately you only have to compete with yourself, not your best friend, not your neighbor, no one.

On the emotional side, get rid of the people that aren't good for you. That has been explored several other times in this book, so I'll refrain from repeating myself. Just remember, when you remove friends, you shouldn't be creating more enemies. You don't have to like the person anymore, but that doesn't mean you have to hate them or wish any harm upon them. You are just doing what is best for you and that means they no longer have an important role, if any, in your life anymore. If they react in a manner which tells you that they think you are enemies now, then that's one them. Continue to keep them separated from you, but if paths cross, which they will, show them respect of civility.

"My stress stresses me out to the point where I'm too stressed to deal with my stress" ~ unknown

You cannot allow yourself to get overwhelmed. Life is far too precious, and it goes by way to quick. You might need to unplug from the world and slow down. No one is so important that they have be reached 24/7. Get away, tune out, forget about the world for a little bit – don't worry, it'll still be there when you come back. Unfuckwithable people can take the stress of the world and life and they can deal with it. They also know how to walk away from it too. When the world is beating you down, are you going lie there and take it or are you going center yourself, recover and rediscover yourself and hit the world back harder?

Stress sucks, and if you don't learn how to cope with it, it will take a physical toll on you. Remember to breathe and that even the darkest or most stressful situations will pass. Offer yourself the chance to escape if need be, and not escape in the sense of running away out of fear, but rather in the way of removing yourself from a situation that has no positive impact on you. If you continually allow the stress of the uncontrollable situations to overtake you, you'll end up either dead or really sick. Being sick, for the most part can be reversable, but sadly, dead is always dead. Don't let the demon of stress take full control of you to the point of no return. You always have the ability to overcome your stresses – it might not be the most popular decision or the choice you want, but it might be what you need.

Winners don't let the world bring them down. They help to bring the world up. Sometimes this philosophy is easier said than done, but it is possible, but you have to be willing to try. There is far too much cynicism in the world today. The world can only be as good as the people that are part of it – not just in it or on it, by part of it. And vice versa, if the world is full of bad people, then you know what you are going to get. When you can look beyond the negatives that flood our perceptions of the world, the world is pretty amazing place. Get out and explore it. You don't have to travel across the globe to faraway places, instead go for hike in a nearby park or reserve. The natural world is beautiful, but the man made one is just as astounding. Explore cities, try those new restaurants, check out the latest live performance – be alive with the world, and the then you'll will see all the good that is available. Unfuckwithable people who win at life can cut through the bullshit and mundane negativity and see that the world can offer endless possibilities. Possibility is a beautiful word, because with it, anything can happen. You are only limited by your own drive and determination. As I've mentioned before, if you really want to do something, you'll find a way; if you don't want to do it, you'll create an excuse.

Final Thoughts:

This book became a labor of love for me. I found that writing this book became therapeutic for myself. I set a goal to write about 1000 words a day, I researched tips for writing and that was like the first one, did I get that, some days yes, some days no. There were also weeks I went without even opening up my files for this book. I also opted to write it how I speak, rather than trying to gussy up the language and make it seem like I'm a lot smarter than I am. The stories and ideas I shared in these pages are hopefully resonating with you. Perhaps you agree with the topics and maybe you disagree. As written in the introduction, I don't care either way, rather I care that you are thinking. Winners are thinkers and thinkers win. When life gets you down, how can you pick yourself up? Are you the type to focus their energies on solving a problem immediately or are the one who will go help others? The concepts discussed should help you or at the most give you a little guidance on how to live a winner's life. Winners don't have to advertise how good they are, rather the air about you should be enough for the world to see. And the world won't remember what you say, but more so what you did. If you think you can't be unfuckwithable, then you're probably right. You must change your mind set on how you live. If you can achieve that, then there is an infinite amount of possibilities for you and your tomorrow.

Command the respect of the people around you, and never tolerate when you are disrespected. Always rise above those who show you disrespect, because you have to remember that they more than likely don't even respect themselves. And if some doesn't have self-respect, they certainly don't deserve any from you. Don't be afraid if people don't like you, who gives a shit – the world really isn't a popularity contest, that should have been left back in high school where you may have been a big fish in a little pond. The real world is a big pond and we are all just little fish, trying to find our way around.

Know and understand your own worth. Never put a price tag on your integrity and hold yourself to the highest standards. When you become the hero in your own story, hopefully you will also inspire others for greatness. Greatness does lie within each of us, but so few of us ever tap into it. You can do practically anything in this life, but if you spend your time complained or stressing out, you'll wake up one day and everything will have passed you by

In closing to my first book, I hope you take something of interest from what has been given to you. Most of the information isn't earth shattering, nor was it hidden. Most of it came from simple research from the internet and additional readings, and just from my own experiences.

Life can be won by everyone, but not everyone wants to win. Some people will always be willing to settle for less than what they deserve. But the moment you start doing that, you will get less than what you deserve. If you want to be unfuckwithable, never settle, always strive for more, but don't live beyond your means. Have passions, have hobbies, be a part of the society you live in. Let your name have meaning when its mentioned when you aren't around.

You don't have to be the Alpha male/female to be unfuckwithable. In essence it's a state of mind, that you hold true to. You don't have to be 6 '5",

275 lbs. of solid muscle to not have been shake your confidence. What you need to be is honest with yourself and the world. You need to let it be known that you although you may not be physically intimidating, that is not an invitation to be a door mat. People shouldn't be able to take advantage you, due to your physical and emotional nature. Unfuckwithable people can stand tall or keep hidden in the shadows. It's how you feel about yourself and not give a crap about what anyone else's things or feels about you, in a negative light. If people love and adore you then yes, hold those feelings dear, but if someone hates you, fine let them hate – work on giving them a reason to hate you more. The greatest revenge you can ever subject an enemy to is to be successful.

There are always going to be bullies – it is naive to think that we can eradicate them through wearing ribbons or special colors or just saying stop. The bully does have a role, much like the lion on the savannah – weed out the weak. This comes from a person who got bullied. I can tell you everything about him, but he doesn't remember me – I was just another kid he messed with. But did I give up, did I cry to my counsellors – NO!!! I busted my ass to make sure I became more than he did. Now he was a head of me in class, I think a junior or senior in high school while I was freshman, so he graduated and I was free. From what I've learned from talking to others that attended school with us, is that after school he made some really poor choices and I think did some time. I on the other hand, went college, learned many skills and become a somewhat successful person. Who really won? I don't think it's me, I know it me. Because he bullied me, I was able to become a better person, so in an ironic turn, I need to thank him. I never said forgive and I can never forget, but I can thank him. Maybe once you read this, you can stand up to your bully or use my story as a starting point to turn your shit around and become successful -and success is really defined by the person working. It doesn't matter if you don't make a fortune, true success comes from being happy with yourself, your life and your choices. Do you have family and friends who would live or die for you? Do you have someone to live and die for? If you answered yes, then you are a winning and when you are winning, you are UNFUCKWITHABLE!!!!

I hope you got something from this read – hopefully it wasn't a long or hard one and maybe it's something you'll reread again and again. Nothing I have talked about is really earth shattering, a lot of it is common sense or stuff you only think about and never say out loud or do in person. The last pages of this book are examples from history from people who were bad ass and unfuckwithable way before those words existed and my own pillars of being unfuckwithable – the outline for most of this book.

Good luck in your life and go win!!!!!!

I don't know what will happen with this book, if I publish it or not, but if you're this far, then I took that step. Who knows when inspiration will strike again, so Ill leave it with a possible, to be continued....

n. kreamer

      The next couple pages are codes throughout the ages. People from different cultures and different time periods, but their base are all so similar. If these peoples who never knew each other can create such similar paths, why can't you? The Pillars are my own list and are what really got me onto the path of this book. I started with I think like 30 and I had them hang in classroom, under the name of "The Toa of Mr. Kreamer" and I'd encourage my students to read them, to remember them and to use them. Over time the list and subsequentially the poster grew bigger and I realized that this could be the basic structure for a book. Now there are over a 100, as of right now, it's a living document, so I plan on adding more but, please don't think you have to follow every single one – its humanly impossible, but if you can take a handful and apply them your ow life, to go forth.

The Pillars of Being Unfuckwithable

1) You can do more than you think. Push yourself
2) You'll never change your life until you change something you do daily
3) If you don't like how things are, change it!!!
4) Sometimes you need to unfollow people in real life
5) Your mindset is everything. What you think, you become
6) You need you, more than you need them. Trust me
7) Don't wait. Life move faster than you think
8) Some people will hate you, let them hate
9) In a world of fish, be a shark
10) If your dreams don't scare you, they aren't big enough
11) The people who want to stay in your life will always find a way

12) Pain can either destroy you or make you stronger

13) Create your future from your future, not your past

14) Money cannot buy happiness, but it sure does afford it

15) When you realize how powerful your words are, you start to be careful with what you say

16) Respect the truth, no matter how hard it is to hear

17) Inspire others to be better versions of themselves

18) When you are wrong, admit it. When you're right, be quiet

19) If it makes you happy, no one's opinion should matter

20) Always work harder than you did yesterday

21) Never let your emotions overpower your intelligence

22) A river cuts through a rock not because of its power, buts its persistence

23) Don't follow the crowd. Make the crowd follow you

24) Be the hero of your own story

25) If you're smart enough, you'll never need to rely on luck

26) Smile big. Laugh often. Never take this life for granted

27) Remember quality over quantity, when dealing with people. It's better to have 4 quarters than 100 pennies.

28) Don't ever lose your spark. We all have a little craziness; it's what can define you.

29) Never let the world change you for the worse. There's far too much cynicism in the world already.

30) There's never a bad time to compliment someone or to tell them you love them; its might be the last thing you say or that they hear

31) Take a chance. The most dangerous two words in the world are "What if...?"

32) Don't let the world change your smile, let your smile change the world

33) Be careful who you trust. Sugar and salt both look the same.

34) Prioritize your time. If you really want to do something, you'll find the time. If you don't want to do something, you'll find an excuse.

35) You cannot change people around you, but you can change the people around you.

36) When faced with a choice between two options, flip a coin. When the coin is in the air, you'll realize which side you want to land up.

37) If someone's presence makes no difference in your life, neither will their absence. This goes for you towards others as well.

38) There are billions of people in the world, and more than 99% of them you don't ever have to worry about meeting. But there will be a select few who you are tied to you. They will cross into your life, back and forth, threading so many knots until they catch, and you finally get it right.

39) There will come a time in your life when you will become infatuated with a single soul. For this person you would do anything and not think twice about it, but when asked why, you will have no answer. You'll try your whole life to understand how a single person can affect you as much as they do, but still you'll find no answer. And no matter how badly you hate it or how

badly it'll hurt, you'll love this person without regret for the rest of your life.

40) Do sharks complain about anything? Work? Mondays? Life? No, there up early, biting stuff, chasing things and constantly reminding the world that they are sharks.

41) Its ok to forgive people, but it's also ok's not to forget either.

42) If you are sure you want to burn a bridge, make sure you leave it in ashes.

43) Worrying, complaining and over-thinking are a lot like rocking in a chair. Sure, they are things to do, but they won't take you anywhere.

44) You will be hurt and not know why. You will hurt others and they won't know why.

45) In life, some days you're the bug, and some days you're the windshield.

46) Don't sweat the small stuff and remember it's all small stuff.

47) Know and respect the value of your time, but never put a price tag on your self-worth.

48) It's all about perspective, to some people you're the hero, to others you might be the villain

49) Don't be afraid to do things alone. If you failed, at least you tried; if you succeed, you don't have to share the credit with anyone.

50) Getting the right answer is great but understanding why it's the right answer is better.

51) Do your best, even if it's not the same as someone else's best.

52) However hard you work and how far you get, there will always be someone willing to do more and go father.

53) It's better to fail at something hard, than to succeed at something easy.

54). Smell good, look good and feel good.

55). Every day try to be the reason someone else smiles.

56) Its ok to be picky about who you let into your circle. Not every person is worthy of your time and energy.

57). No, Mondays do not suck!!

58). Treat everyone from the custodian to the CEO with the same level of respect.

59) Never trust a person who doesn't like dogs but always trust a dog who doesn't like a person.

60) Keep those who matter close to you.

61) Time waits for nobody, but sometimes you may have to wait a long time.

62) You should never have to announce how good you are, how hard you work and anything as such. Your ability and achievements should speak for themselves.

63) Command respect never demand it.

64). A good experience is a great teacher, but a great teacher is an even better experience.

65) It's not having what you want, it's wanting what you've have.

66) Just because today was bad, doesn't tomorrow will be as well. Tomorrow has the possibility of being the greatest day ever.

67)You cannot change the cards your dealt, just how you play the hand

68) There's a very fine line between arrogance and confidence. Always know which side of that line you're on

69) Doing nothing changes nothing

70) Sometimes our silence can be the loudest voice we have.

71) History is always written by the winner

72) There's always the good reason, and then there's the "real" reason.

73) It's not being selfish for wanting to be treated well.

74) You become the master of your own life when you learn to control where your attention goes.

75) What other people think of you is none of your business.

76) No matter how far down the wrong path you've travelled, there's always time to turn around.

77) Never be controlled by people, money or your past mistakes.

78) It's better to burn out than to fade away

79) You can't spend all your time thinking about the future, or else you'll forget about living in the "now"

80) Anybody who ever made you think you weren't good enough, was wrong, they weren't good enough for you.

81) The sun is going to rise, and tomorrow will happen, whether you are part of it or not.

82) Be so good, that you can't be ignored

83). You have to hate losing more than you love winning

84). You judge your own character by the quality of people you surround yourself with

85). If you can't be trusted with a secret, then you probably shouldn't trust others with yours

86). In life, you will be many things and different people to everyone you meet

87) Every scar, either physical or emotional, always has a story behind. Don't judge others to quickly.

88). Don't begrudge others for having more than you. You don't know what they may have had to sacrifice for it.

89) We don't stop playing because we grow, we grow old because we stop playing

90) Your value doesn't decrease based on someone's inability to see your worth

91) Keep yourself educated, because stupid people are lot easier to control.

92) Anything worth doing, is worth doing correctly and fully.

93) Always know your rights, but also always know your responsibilities

94) Never be afraid to lend a helping hand, but never forget that 2nd place is still the first loser.

95) Loyalty is always worth more than its weight in gold

96) Be the person that both your parents and your children would be proud of, and be the type of friend you'd be honored to have.

97) If you're going to do something, do it with passion

98). We all have a time machine of our own. When we travel back, those are memories and dreams take us to our future.

99) Control your fears or they will control you

100) Be gracious in both victory and defeat

101) Never announce your next move, always keep others guessing and never let them see where you're coming from or going to.

102) Stay low key. Not everyone needs to know everything about you.

103) If you refuse to learn to heal from any past trauma and choose to just accept it, because "that's who I am" then YOU are your own problem

104) Don't be afraid to start over. It's a chance to build something better this time.

105) People will either compliment your life or complicate it. Know the difference

106) Help others, even if no one is helping you

107) Learn to be open minded. You might be enthusiastic in your beliefs, so expect others to be with theirs, as well. Have open conversations and learn how to agree to disagree.

108) Privacy is power. People cannot ruin what they do not know

109) Celebrate the achievements of others. Never be upset if a friend gets ahead

110) Never deal in empty threats, only deal with full promises.

111) If it doesn't improve your life, it doesn't belong in your life

112). It's better to be hated for being who you are, then love for being someone you aren't.

113) An ugly truth is always better than a beautiful lie.

114) It's always better to be the lonely lion than the popular sheep

115) Some people are just horrible; there is no use in searching for the good in them

116) We might look different and think different, but in the end, we are all waves from the same ocean.

117) Inspire in others, the same greatness they may see within you

118) There are people you need in your life, there are people you want in your life and then there are people who are your life. Make sure they are all the same people.

119)Always surround yourself with people who can you at your worst and still make you think you're the best, not the other way around.

120) Keep a small circle. Those in it should be your biggest supports. They should cheer the loudest for your successes and help hold you up during your failures. If your circle doesn't do this, the answer is simple: You need a different circle.

121) In the end, all you need to do in this life is to try to be the reason someone else smiles. With any luck, they'll be the reason you smile too.

122) Just because someone disagrees with you, doesn't mean they hate you. You can have different opinions and thoughts and still get along and respect each other.

123) Be careful with your words. Choose them wisely. In the heat of the moment, your words can cause severe damage. "The axe always forgets, but the tree always remembers."

124) Be kind. For no other reason than to be kind. Be kind. And expect nothing in return for it. If its reciprocated, accept it and move forward. If it isn't, accept that and move forward and continue being kind.

The Knights Code

1) Love the Lord Your God with all your heart, soul, mind, and strength
2)   Obey those in authority over you
3)   Stand against injustice and evil
4)   Defend the weak and protect them
5)   Respect the home of women

6)   Refrain from wanton giving of offence

7)   Speak the truth at all times

8)   Be generous and wiling o share

9)   Persevere and finish the task at hand

10) Pursue excellence in all you do

The Warrior Code

Honour

You will uphold what is just. You will perform your duty with integrity, uprightness and trustworthiness

Courage

You will face danger, fear and changing circumstances with self-possession, confidence and resolution. You will be brave in both mind and spirit

Mercy

When not in combat, no matter how provoked you will forbear to inflict harm when you have the power to inflict it. When it is within your power you will offer compassionate treatment of an adversary or offender. When it is within you power you will off clemency

Loyalty

You will be faithful to your commitments and obligations. You will be faithful to the Warrior Code

Fidelity

You will observe all promises and duties made as a Warrior. Failure will mean breaking your faith in your belief and the Warrior Code

Honesty

You will refrain from lying, cheating or stealing

Above all else a Warrior must value the Warrior Code. Failure to do so will result in banishment from the Warrior Class

Virtues of Ancient Rome

Dignitas

Dignity, a sense of self-worth, personal pride

Gravitas

Gravity, knowing the importance of the matter at hand

Pietas

Dutifulness, piety, devotion, respect for the natural order

Humanitas

Refinement, learning, culture, civility

Veritas

Truthfulness, honesty in dealing with others

Aequitas

Equity, impartiality, fair dealing

Nobilitas

Nobility, noble action

Liberalitas

Liberality, generosity, open mindedness

Firmitas

Tenacity, strength of mind, the ability to stick to a purpose

Comitas

Humor, ease of manner, openness and friendliness

NINE NOBLE VIRTUES (CELTIC)

COURAGE

I face my fear and defend my family and kindred from all dangers

DISCIPLINE

I do what is necessary and right on my own accord, without bribe or threat

FIDELITY

I am true to family, friends, kindred and those who I pledge my service

HONOR

I stand by my oaths and honor my ancestors by keeping my name pure among the kindred

HOSPITALITY

I share hearth, food and drink with my friends, my kindred, and the weary traveler at my door

INDUSTRIOUS

I take joy in labor and hold nothing back from the work I pledge to do

PERSEVERANCE

I press on against all odds until my goal is met, the task is finished, and I have done all said I will do

SELF-RELIANCE

I learn skills and grow strong so that I may learn my way in the worlds and be no burden to others

THE BUSHIDO CODE

Gi – Integrity

- Be acutely honest throughout your dealings with all people. Believe in justice, not from other people, but from yourself. To the true warrior, all points of view are deeply considered regarding honesty, justice, and integrity. Warrior make a full commitment to their decisions

Rei – Respect

- True warriors have no reason to be cruel. The do not need to prove their strength. Warriors are courteous even to their enemies. Warriors are only respected for their strength in battle, but also by their dealings with others. The true strength of a warrior becomes apparent during difficult time

Yu – Heroic Courage

- Hiding like a turtle in a shell is not living at all. A true warrior must have heroic courage. It is absolutely risky. It is living life completely, fully, and wonderfully. Heroic courage is not blind. It is intelligent and strong

Meiyo – Honor

- Warriors have only one judge of honor and character and this is themselves. Decisions they make and how these decisions are carried out is a reflection of whom they truly are. You cannot hide from yourself

Jin – Compassion

- Through intense training and hard work, the true warrior becomes quick and strong. They are not like most people. They develop a power that must be used for good. They have compassions. They help their fellow man when given the chance. If an opportunity does not arise, they go out of their way to find one

Makoto – Honesty and Sincerity

- When warriors say that they will perform an action, it is as good as done. Nothing will stop them from completing what they say they will do. They do not have to "give their word." They do not have to "promise". Speaking and doing are the same action.

Chu – Duty and Loyalty

- Warriors are responsible for everything that they have done and everything that they have said and all of the consequences that follow. They are immensely loyal to all of those in their care. To everyone that they are responsible for, the remain fiercely true.

7-5-3 CODE

7 VIRTUES OF A WARRIOR

Rectitude

Courage

Benevolence

Politeness/Propriety

Honesty/Sincerity

Honor

Loyalty

5 KEYS TO HEALTH

Rational Nutrition

Sensible Exercise

Efficient Rest

Proper Hygiene

Positive Attitude

3 STATES OF MIND

Zanshin – Alertness, Awareness

Mushin – Clear Mind

Fudoshin – Emotional Balance

Made in the USA
Middletown, DE
29 July 2020